WAKE UP
It's Time to Dream!

JOSÉ TORRÓN

GBH
Books

Translator: Ryan Keller
Editor: F. Nitch and M. Weiner
Managing Editor: Manuel Aleman
Designer: Tina Conti

Published in the United States by CBH Books.
CBH Books is a division of Cambridge BrickHouse, Inc.
Cambridge BrickHouse, Inc.
855 Turnpike Street, Suite 237
North Andover, MA 01845
U.S.A.

Library of Congress Catalog No. 2017942700
ISBN 978-1-59835-471-3
First Edition
Printed in U.S.A.
10 9 8 7 6 5 4 3 2 1

For Isa

*I thank my mother who gave me life,
and who has always been present in every
important moment of my existence.
I thank my wife Ive, because every day
is a celebration with her.*

Prologue

A significant contribution to the movement of human potential, José Torrón shares in this book conversations that become opportunities for readers to take action. I know him personally and see his ongoing efforts and skill for contributing generously; this work is evidence of that. I urge you to take advantage of his knowledge.

—*John Hanley, PhD*

Contents

Chapter 1

Think, Feel, and Speak Only About What You Want to Live...

Thoughts become a reality. Thoughts are pure creative energy. What you are thinking is manifesting in your life as your reality. If you have thoughts of joy, your life will be in peace. If in your mind there is conflict and criticism, your life will be full of conflict and criticism.

The same thing happens with money. If you are constantly thinking about debts and how to pay them, that is what you will be experiencing. You have probably already accumulated several debts and anguished over how to pay for them.

What you are thinking, you are expanding and manifesting into your reality. It is very important to be acutely aware in each moment that the process of creating our outcomes begins in our mind; it starts with what we are thinking. The trick is to be aware and choose thoughts that give you power, thoughts that create what you want to live, instead of what you do not want to live, always choosing thoughts with the power of creating your dreams.

I invite you to look at the things you do not like about yourself, your life and what you are thinking about them; what your interpretation is of all this.

I have a private practice for coaching, and during the first conversations I have with the people I coach, I invite them to begin thinking only about what they want to see in their lives, what they would like to live and the future that they are dreaming of. *I tell them to truly stop their minds and look into their hearts: how do they really, really, really want to live their lives. More so, I invite them to write out their future just as they want to live it, in as much detail as possible.* They need to permit themselves to write how they want to live, standing from a place of freedom and abundance; from a mental space where everything is entirely possible, permitting themselves to dream these things that they really, really, really want to live. When that happens, their life will never be the same.

It starts with this simple step: they sit in a room, alone, pen and paper in hand, writing, writing, writing and writing absolutely everything that comes to their minds and hearts; everything they would like to live; every one of their goals and dreams. And that very exercise of being alone with themselves and writing, without interruptions from phone calls or the television, is powerful enough to change their lives forever.

A phrase I use is: *"Think, sit, and speak only about what you want to live."* Your words have a lot of power for creation. Everything begins there: *in the word.* If you are speaking of things you do not want to experience, probably in your life there are things you do not want. If you are talking about what you want to live, it is very possible that you have already shared the things you do like. And when I tell you to talk about the things you want, it is not necessary for these words to come out of your mouth.

The internal, private dialogue within your mind; that "little voice" that always has its opinion about everything (right now as you read this book, that "little voice" is giving you its opinion), *that "little voice"* is having a profound impact on what you are living. And that "little voice" is the silent narration of your future. Your private conversations become public by way of your results. In other words, there are no real private conversations; everything is seen in your results. Everything you think is manifesting itself. *You live out what you thought.* You have gotten to this point in your life through your conversation. *You have thought up your life.*

Some people have learned to be so negative that they prevent new and beautiful things from coming into their lives. Why? Because we have been born in a historic moment in which most of the collective conversations we receive from the entire world are negative. Newspapers, television, the Internet, radio: they are full of news about murders, robberies and human tragedies of pain, hopelessness and simply *"not being able to;"* that *"things used to be easier."* That conversation that comes out of the mouths of millions of people is transmitted from generation to generation and is repeated by those of us who are alive now. And so, it repeats and repeats, and our conversations continue to manifest themselves.

Let us imagine for a moment that we have a device that measures conversations and that we have it connected to the planet. If the device could classify the "positive" or "negative" conversations, we would prove that 80% of them are negative. Worst of all is that we do not even realize this, and future generations are going to hear these same conversations. Perhaps, even worse every time they are repeated. I'm not saying this to create despair. Quite the contrary: this is so we become aware of what we are talking about and that we are transmitting this to future generations.

This book is written with a focus contrary to what most people have heard for a long time. This book covers:

possibility,

love,

faith,

faith in yourself,

being positive,

absolute certainty,

that it does not matter where you are coming from and what has happened in your life,

today you can begin to design your future,

that it is possible,

that you can do it,

that today, at this moment,

you can feel differently;

that, now, things can be different forever,

that your life experience can be a good one.

Today, thinking, feeling and speaking about what you want, you can change your life. A few days ago, I was listening to a 20-year-old young man talk about how he saw his life. He left me with my mouth wide open when he told me "Most people say they don't know how their future is going to be, but I can see my future; I know how my future is going to be."

It's all up to me.
It's about going to the future
with all of your heart,
with your mind,
with your being
and daring to say "yes."
That "Yes, I can create what
I'm dreaming about,
yes, I can!"

You can be who you have not yet been; you can have what you have not yet had; you can become someone you have not yet become. It is possible for everything in your heart to happen.

Everything begins with a thought.
Everything is absolutely possible.

Chapter 2

If You Can Dream It, You Can Create It...

Everything around you was impossible before one person, or several people, committed themselves to making them happen.

It's not that they merely "wanted to,"

but that they committed themselves to these things.

A few days ago, I read an analogy about *"wanting something"* and *"committing to something."* For example, if you are served eggs and bacon for breakfast, the chicken *"wanted"* because it contributed to the meal, but the little pig *"committed,"* by giving its life. "Committing" is when your entire life is at stake. Your whole body is committed, not just a part of it.

In less than sixty years, the human race has gone from the first sustained flight to landing on the moon in a spaceship. Just a few years ago, someone with heart problems had no choice but to live with their illness until death came along. Today, we can have heart transplants. The mobile phone you have in your pocket is like something out of a science fiction movie. In fact, the first one I saw was on the *Star Trek* television series.

Today you can communicate with the entire world in an instant, and with your phone, you can search information around the world in just a few seconds. You can simultaneously buy discount airfare, watch an action movie, take a selfie, receive thousands of job offers by email, have 12 clocks with 12 time zones, listen to music, measure your heartbeat, have a GPS, etc. All of this from the comfort of your chair! All of this was impossible not too long ago.

The same thing happens in your life. Things that have been impossible for you are impossible to achieve until you think they are possible.

Everything you wish for at this moment,
all of it is entirely possible!
You are a thought away from achieving it;
you are a "yes" away from making it so.

If that desire is in your heart, it is because of something; from where did it come? It's time to be daring; the time to tell yourself yes to that which is in your heart.

What you think about has a lot of power. Your thoughts and mine are made of the same thing that the entire universe is made of: *energy!*

If you took a super-powered microscope and began to look within yourself at what you have done, you will see your cells, then your atoms, then your electrons, protons, and neutrons. If you could go deeper and further into your microscopic world and look for more, you will find your energy in the form of quarks and empty space. If you take a photo camera and were thrown out and you enter from one end of an atom until you come out of the other, and during the entire time you took photos and videos, all of the images will be blank and the only thing there will be energy.

We are a manifestation of the energy, just like the energy that you are thinking about, just like the energy that is being manifested in the universe.

When words come out of my mouth, that logically come from my thoughts, thoughts that we know are pure creative energy, I am creating my reality.

If I am talking trash, what do you think I am going to create?

If I am talking about possibility, abundance, faith, what do you think I am manifesting? What do you think you are going to manifest?

The same thing happens with visual information, the images that are reaching my mind. If I listen to and watch trash, what do you think my mind will be expanding? And when I talk about this, it's not necessarily a conscious process. When you fill your mind with things, these things tend to expand and manifest in your life. Take care of what enters your mind. It's like when you eat; if you fill your body with healthy food, then what you manifest is health. But if you fill it with harmful and toxic things, then that is what you are going to manifest.

It is entirely possible to alter what is happening in your life in all areas. What you are living today is the result of the decisions and actions that your thoughts have generated. But I have good news for you: the universe is not static, and you are not destined to live anything that is currently happening in your life. Your life is not a photograph, but instead a movie. What would the title be of the movie of your life today? What is the title that you want for the movie of your life tomorrow?

The first step is to alter and change what is

happening, seeing what you are thinking about the things you want to have, attract and manifest.

Begin to think of things
that you do want to live.

Sometimes it's hard if you are immersed in situations like debt, conflict, and trying emotional problems. But if you are committed to making a quantum leap:

You need to stop at this moment
and take action.
Dearest friend,
No one is going to live your life for you,
no one is going to open your business for you,
no one is going to save money for you,
no one, no matter how much they love you,
is going to do the things you need to create the life
you are dreaming of,
and you are just a thought away
from achieving it.

The game goes even further on. The beliefs that are in your mind, in your subconscious, also expand powerfully. The worst thing is we don't even realize that these beliefs are there and are manifesting themselves. Until you manage to see and change these beliefs, they will be manifesting themselves in your life, and you will call it fate. It's like that Julio Iglesias song that says *"I've stumbled over the same stone again."* The stone will not move until you move it, but it is not in front of you. Instead, it is inside of you. That stone is imaginary, but you are giving it the power to be real. And since you have spent so much time thinking about it, since it's a chronic thought, you have believed that this thought is real. But it is only a thought. And it is a negative thought! Don't pay much attention to what you are thinking; they are only thoughts. Question everything you think as much as you can, even if it's only once in your life, question everything, everything you are thinking.

Imagine that you are a new computer and what you install on the hard drive are computer games, and there are zombies and cybernetic soldiers in all of them that are wanting to finish you off. Every time you turn on your computer, what do you think you'll find on it? Even if you look for a game where it is possible to be happy, and you can manifest abundance, you won't be able to find it. The code does not exist; the program is not on the computer.

The same thing happens with your mind and mine. Somehow, we generate the programming that we have at this moment, and we are planting the seeds that we will see in the future.

Your thoughts are the silent declaration
of the future of your life.

In fact, since you are already reading this book, you are somehow aware and are becoming aware, that, from this very moment, everything can be different. From this moment, you no longer need to store information that you do not want. A lot of information will come along that doesn't even belong to you, but you'll decide if you keep those thoughts or not.

What programming is on your hard drive that makes your life appear as it does? It is time to stop and choose what thoughts you are going to have. It is time to be silent and see, just see what you are thinking about in all areas of your life. It can be helpful to write down all of the beliefs you find, all of the memories of when you lived in abundance, all of the memories you find that brought you to where you are today.

"Just Do It!"

"Just Do It" from Nike, is one of the most powerful ad campaigns I have ever seen. There you have the secret to manifest what you want; to manifest everything you want. How do you do it? By doing it! There are infinite ways to generate and manifest everything you want, but if you don't get up from your chair and take action, nothing will happen.

No one,

no one,

no one,

no one,

no one will do it for you.

This is your life.

You are the pilot.

You are the one writing the script,

you are the leading actor.

You can keep arguing with the excuses that you have learned. It's very simple: either you're living the outcome you want, or you're supporting the reason to justify why you're not living what you want. If you are not committed to taking action, I understand that reading the rest of this book is going to be a waste of time for you.

Take action!

Remember that you were born with a clean computer hard drive and you filled it with information or it was filled for you. This information is what is generating the excuses, and if you are reading this book, I know that somehow you are sick or "Capital S Sick" of things not happening in your life.

So, stand up and take action.
Perhaps it's time:
to enroll in college,
start your new business,
visit your loved ones,
heal relationships and get closer,
pay off your debts for good,
take the vacations that never come,
paint that portrait,
put that 'For Sale' sign on your house
and move to another country,
buy the sailboat you have always dreamed of.
You know what you want to do.
Only you know what really moves you.
In the end, you know better than anyone.
You are an expert when it comes to you.

Today you have one day less than yesterday; if your life was to end right now, what things will go with you? What things did you not experience because you were too busy working to pay bills?

Just do it!
If you don't do it, who will?

If you don't do it now, when?
You are one hundred percent responsible for everything
occurring in your life.
This means you can alter
the course of your life forever if you stop
and take responsibility for everything,
all of your outcomes,
your emotions,
everything.
Go for it!

Chapter 3
Do What You Like...

Yesterday, I saw on the Internet a young man with Down Syndrome that does a happy dance when he goes in his restaurant every morning because he is delighted to be able to do what he does. This young man is the owner, and in addition to the dance he does (which I believe is spectacular to start the day that way), he also hugs all of his clients. He calls himself the hugging machine. Wow! Imagine starting your days like that; every morning dancing just because, and embracing the people that are close to you: your family, your colleagues, your clients, everyone...It's magic.

You already are where you are. It is what it is. Can you change your past? Nope...

But you have the gift that you are still alive, and you can change your future forever. You can invent yourself today, something different that you would like to live and create. Now!

The way in which I'm going to invite you to do this is *declaring what you do want to live.* Notice that it says *what you "want" to live.* This is of vital importance. *Stop doing things you don't want to do.*

This does not mean you should become an irresponsible person, but:

if you do not like the job you have,

it is time to change it;

if you want to emigrate to another country,

it's time to use that passport;

if what you are living is somehow not really what you like,

what moves you,

what you are passionate about,

it is time to change things;

and if you need to change it all,

then it is time to take action and change everything.

Your life is running out.

Today you have one day less than yesterday.

No matter how much you live your life, the day of your death will still be too soon.

If you are gifted 80 years of life,
you will only live 29,200 days.

When I declare something, in this very moment, I begin to manifest it. The energy of my thought begins to expand. When I say it, I declare it with strength, with absolute certainty; I write it, I bring it from an invisible plane to a visible plane. It exists. Everything around you has begun to manifest itself from the invisible to the visible plane through a declaration.

Everything: The car you drive (if you drive a car), your house, the planes that cross the sky, the watch you have on your wrist, the computer from where I am writing this for you, the glasses I use to correct my eyesight, the shoes you have on, everything, absolutely everything, everything, everything that humankind has manifested in these millions of years that we are walking on the Earth, began with a *declaration.*

When I declare something, I open a possibility that did not exist at all, I open a space for new creation; I open a door to my future that was closed, or better yet, did not exist. And the only reason it exists is that I am declaring it, I am saying it, I am bringing it from the invisible to the visible plane. You send an order to the future to manifest what you want; you send a bolt of energy to the future for what you need to happen, to awaken, and begin to move towards the direction where it will be manifested. But I invite you to declare without seeking the how. I welcome you to declare by opening this new space of creation. A space from which I can see opportunities, ideas, and new things. A space from where I can stand and create. It is not about a process of questions and answers; it is about a new space that opens and where I am aware; a space where I am aware of my declaration and the infinite possibilities that exist in this moment in the universe for me.

It's like a video game: when you turn on a video game, even though it's you pushing the control buttons, all of the moves already exist. It's the same if you turn to the right or towards the left, either will happen, since the possibility within the video game was programmed. The universe is programmed to manifest all of your moves. But you need to play them to see them manifested. When you go from one world to the other, that possibility already exists. If you stay with the declaration, if you stay in that space of possibility as if it were a possibility, you are going to be conscious of the different and infinite worlds that are always available.

Your declarations should always be made from a context of absolute certainty; believe, but truly believe that it is so, that it will be different from the reality that you are living, the reality that you are creating, that you are manifesting.

If you don't believe it's possible,

it's not going to happen!

Stop not believing in yourself.

Repeat to yourself again and again:

I can!

I can!

I can!

Shout it if you need to:

I caaaaaaaaaannn!!!

It's possibleeeeee!!!

It is going to require a lot of energy from you at the beginning, since you have probably been in the same zone for a long time: *your comfort zone.* It's like a plane during take-off; it needs all of its thrust to take off and then it is easier. It's like laying down in a hammock for a long time. Is it easy or hard to get out of the hammock? In the same manner, it will require effort at the beginning.

Stand up from that chair; take action.

If it is hard for you, it is because you have been submerged in a painful reality for some time. Well, whatever it is, it is possible to change it all at this moment.

If you still are not certain that you are going to change, OK, that's fine, keep doing it, writing it, *declaring it!* Until an absolute certainty is born within you, until you generate a powerful internal dialogue with yourself that:

Yes, it will happen,

yes, you can,

it is already happening.

If it gets hard,

do it even though it is hard.

If you don't have the certainty that it is possible,

do it without certainty.

If you don't make it on the first try,

you'll get it on the second

or the third.

Don't quit!

No one can do it for you,

only you can manifest your life.

Only you can start your business,

only you can heal your family,

only you can have the extraordinary couple's relationship, only you can take your vacations.

It's possible.

It's possible.

It's possible.

Don't quit.

If not you, whom?

If not now, when?

Think of your vision every day,

create a system that works for you,

write it everywhere,

tell everyone

talk about it,

talk about it,

talk about it.

Tell the whole world,

put up photos,

clippings for you to see every day

of what you want.

For example, if you want a house, look for magazines that have photos of homes like the one you're dreaming of, cut out the pictures and paste them everywhere. I invite you to make a poster of your vision. Look for some poster board and fill it with photos and clippings of *everything you want to live.*

For the money you want to have, write a check with the amount, print images of bills; be *specific* with the amount. If you want a beautiful home, paste photos of houses. If you want happiness for your family, paste pictures of happy people.

After making your vision board, stand in front of it and don't think of anything; just look at the images and fill your mind with everything you do want. Do this with as much time and as often as possible every day. What you are doing with this is telling your subconscious:

"Hey, get to work,
this is what we're going to live."

Your subconscious begins to generate the ideas and the ways, awakening areas of your mind that were dormant. In this manner, you are going to force your brain to become active. We use about 5% of this super-mega computer that is our mind. Put your vision board in a place you pass by frequently. I have my vision board in my room, and I see it every time I get up, brush my teeth, and lie down. Also, I fill the mirrors of my home with written declarations. *Ha ha ha,* sometimes, if my wife and I want to comb our hair at the same time, there's not enough space in the mirror.

Become a creative machine of your life. Don't

lose a second. When I declare, I open an empty space. A space where there was nothing before. A space where everything is possible. This vision board brings together the declarations of images of your dreams. I invite you to feel them every time you are in front of them. Feel as if they have already happened.

When you stand in the empty space, the only thing that exists is *possibility*. It is like standing in front of a blank canvas. You can paint the portrait that you want; you can use the colors that you want. Out of nothing, everything is possible. Everything you see around you, everything, has been manifested out of nothing.

Impossible is just a word, an opinion. Generally, the people who have not attained what you want to achieve will say that it is impossible. Whoever wants to pull you down is perhaps below you. If you now want to manifest a million dollars and you go and ask the people who have not manifested this, that don't have that amount in a bank account, what do you think their answer will be?

But if you go and ask people who do have a million dollars or more in an account, what do you think they're going to say about whether it's possible or not?

When Christopher Columbus went on his

voyage, everyone thought the Earth was flat and that he was crazy.

When the Wright brothers went from making bicycles to making airplanes, they were crazy.

Before Roger Bannister had run a mile in less than four minutes, it was humanly impossible. And it was the mind that made it possible.

Treat your thoughts with love. Choose what you think about. Your thoughts are the future of your life. What you think about, you will live, like it or not. In the beginning, it can be hard, but it is a matter of practice, like riding a bicycle. If you ride a bike, the first times are uncomfortable, but as soon as you become used to it, it comes naturally. It's like driving a car, which is very awkward at the beginning; you're scared of crashing; you forget about the gear shift; you forget to look in the rear-view mirror. But then it is as if the car were an extension of your body; it comes naturally. The same thing will happen to you with your thoughts:

Train yourself to think about what you want to live,

train yourself to think about what you really like.

Talk about what you want to live,not what you don't want.

Think, feel and talk about what you want to live.

A recommendation is for you to meet with people

that have already manifested or are manifesting the things you want. Meet with people that say yes. For example, if you want to manifest money and you see that all of the friends with whom you spend time are penniless, it is the time to include people who have money in that group that you talk and spend time with. It is not about not loving the friends with less money than you; that's not what I am saying. Keep loving your people and spending time with them, but include people in your life that have manifested that which you are in the process of manifesting.

Just a few days ago I was listening to a CD by Les Brown, an author I very much like and admire, and he said that the person who earns $200,000 a year does not have much to talk about with the person who makes $20,000 a year. There's nothing wrong with either of them, just that the context that they have created is different and this will generate different conversations. If you want to be a two hundred thousand dollars a year person, it's time to make time in your agenda for another group of people as well.

Friend,
you need to truly be hungry,
really hungry for this to happen.
If you don't have a hunger for something to happen,
it won't happen.

I invite you to truly look in your heart for that which you enjoy and dedicate your time to it.

If something really, really doesn't motivate you,

don't waste your time on it.

You are going to find a ton of excuses along the way to not achieve those things,

or if you manage to achieve them,

I don't think you'll find meaning when you're there.

Find the purpose for which you came to this life.

No one has ever been,

is or will be the same as you.

You are a unique being.

What are you doing here?

If you don't know, that's fine.

But at least look in your heart:

What do you find fulfilling?,

what catches your attention?,

what do you like?,

and start there.

And if you don't find it,

make something up and move!

Find a dream that keeps you up at night.

Your life begins after a 'yes.'

Chapter 4

It Can be Easy, Spontaneous and Continuous…

What comes to your mind when you read the word "desert"? The word "desert" brings to mind heat, sun, loneliness, hunger, thirst, pain, sand, and death. What happens to a person when you leave them in the desert for a month without supplies? This person is going to experience everything that we mentioned, right? And, what happens if we leave a thousand people in the desert, one after another? They will all probably have the same experience. Why does this happen? Because the context of a "desert" always produces the same result.

The context in people are the *beliefs* that this person has. It doesn't matter where you take them geographically, their context will produce the same outcome.

If someone believes that things are resolved with fists, how do you think that person is solving the conflicts in his life? With his fists. And what happens if you take this person to New York, Belize, China, or Australia? How do you think this person is going to solve his problems in these countries?

The context produces the content that manifests itself in your life. If your life is easy-going and fun, your beliefs, no matter where you are, even if you are imprisoned, will produce a similar life experience, wherever we put your body.

A few years ago, I knew of a person who won 16 million dollars in the lottery and two years later was signing bad checks. The context creates and manifests the content.

There are people who manage to get in a bad mood and fight or get depressed in Disney World. When I was small, I was on vacation with my family and several other families, close to us, and one of the adult couples were fighting most of the trip. The fight had nothing to do with Mickey or Pluto.

You'll tell me "Ok, ok, I understand. What I know, my *context*, is producing my content, what I am living."

"And how do I change my context, José?"

The context is always created.
It is not learned, it is not an accident,
it is not a casualty,
it is not random.
The context is created.
There are many ways to create my context.

One of them is exposing yourself to new information like what you're reading here. There is a lot of printed and digital news, on TV, in videos, that can help you modify your context, to modify what you know.

Find a coach or several coaches

Nine years ago, for the first time in my life, I hired a person I admire to train me about life. It's as if I was a football player and my coach showed me the areas where I needed to move differently. The coaching session was powerful; by having it and allowing myself to explore it and take specific actions, I managed to move my life in that direction.

Create a support group

Come together with people that say yes; a group of people that are not necessarily your family. In fact, I recommend that they are not family members since you will probably talk about similar things with them. Open yourself to bringing new ideas, listening to new opinions, to having new conversations.

Declare what you want to live

When you declare new things that you have not lived, your limiting beliefs about these declarations come out. At that moment, you become conscious of those beliefs (of the context in which you are operating), and you can change them for others if they help you to manifest those dreams.

Stop defending your opinion, let go of being right

What you know is your context, and your context is manifesting what your life contains. If you don't take away anything else from this book, just this last point, you won't need anything else to transform your life forever. Let go of what you know. What you know and the interpretation that you give to what happens in your life is the fruit of the context from where you are operating.

What you see isn't, it's just what you see

Your best way of thinking is keeping you in the life you're living.

It's time for your life to be easy, spontaneous and continuous. For that to happen, you need to change your context. It's time to change what you know. Once you change your context, you will always manifest the things you want to live from the "easy, spontaneous and continuous" perspective.

A happy person,

always manifests happiness.

A wealthy person,

always manifests wealth.

A fun person

is always having fun.

The context always creates the content.

Whether you want to or not,

you are manifesting your life.

Whether you want to or not,

the universe is giving you what you ask for.

Whether you want to or not,

you are going to live what you are thinking,

feeling and talking about.

Chapter 5

I Don't Know that I Don't Know: Where Miracles Happen...

There are three areas of knowledge from where you can manifest your future:

I know that I do know.

I know that I don't know.

I don't know that I don't know.

The first knowledge space from where you can create your future we'll call:

I know that I do know

Everything you know, everything you have learned since you were born, all of the things that you have been exposed to, everything you have felt, everything you remember, everything you have interpreted and are interpreting of what you have lived is *I know that I do know.* From there, you can create your life. What you can create by operating from that space you are probably already living in your life. There is nothing wrong with that. But if you continue creating from what you know, it will look similar to what you already have. You're going to have a little more, you're going to create a little more. You're going to achieve a little more.

The next knowledge space from which you can manifest your life is:

I know that I don't know

I know that I don't know how to speak Mandarin, but I can learn to speak Mandarin and from there create new things.

I know that I don't know how to fly an airplane, but I can learn to fly and use the knowledge acquired to manifest new things in my life.

There are many things that I am aware of that I have not mastered that I do not know for the creation of my future, but I can learn to master that knowledge and use it in the creation of my future. That space is probably broader than what *I know that I do know.* I can expand my knowledge, take classes, enroll in an educational program and expose myself to new information and learn to use it in the manifestation of my future.

I don't know that I don't know

This is the space where the magic in your life happens. To access this space of knowledge, I need to *declare* through my words and stand in a new space that did not exist, a precognitive space (before a thought arrives) and stay in that space of absolute possibility; a space where I enter blankly, not seeking answers. A space where I enter to realize, to become aware; a creative space where I stand to see and recognize things. We have been there unconsciously many times.

I know we have all had experiences in which we declare something, and it happens sooner than we thought; we simply found the way; we knew how it was. In this space, *I manifest what I am.* In the creative space of *I don't know that I don't know,* everything has always existed. Everything you want, every impossible goal for you and me, already exists; it's just that we haven't entered into that creative space yet, and we have not yet identified how to make our dreams manifest themselves easily, spontaneously and continuously.

The universe manifests

itself easily.

The universe manifests

itself spontaneously.

The universe manifests

itself continuously.

About this edition:
"Wake Up, It's Time to Dream!"
by José Torrón
Produced by the publishing house CBH Books
(Massachusetts, United States),
Year 2017.
For any comment on this work
or permission request, you can write to:
Spanish Department
Cambridge BrickHouse, Inc.
855 Turnpike Street, Suite 237
North Andover, MA 01845
U.S.A.

www.ingramcontent.com/pod-product-compliance
Lightning Source LLC
Chambersburg PA
CBHW071651040426
42452CB00009B/1828